Victorian Walks on the

Book 1: Ryde, Newport, Cowes, Goasnill, Newtown, Yarmouth, Freshwater and The Needles

In the late 19th century, Britain's middle class enjoyed greater leisure time and disposable income than previous generations, enabling families to travel further afield for day trips and holidays. The Isle of Wight was easily accessible from southern England by taking a train to Portsmouth or Southampton and then crossing the Solent by 'steamer' to Ryde or Cowes. The transport network on the island was well-developed and it was possible to reach almost every town and village by train, horse-drawn coach or coastal ferry.

Detailed guide books were available to help tourists make the most of their visit and this booklet reproduces text from 'Black's Guide to the Isle of Wight', published in 1883. It includes information about transport services but the author assumes that readers will walk to the 'attractions' he describes, taking in the scenery as they ramble. Accordingly, he explains where to go, how to get there, what to look for and provides the history of places visited. This booklet covers the north and west coasts and most of the central, inland area. Book 2 focuses on the south coast from Freshwater Gate through Brixton, Chale, Ventnor, Shanklin and Sandown to Brading.

The nine photographs are from the Keasbury-Gordon Photograph Archive and date from the 1880s to the 1920s.

The text is remarkably detailed and enables us to travel back in time to visit this delightful, historically important, British isle. I hope you enjoy the journey.

Andrew Gill

King Edward VII 'going on board' at Cowes

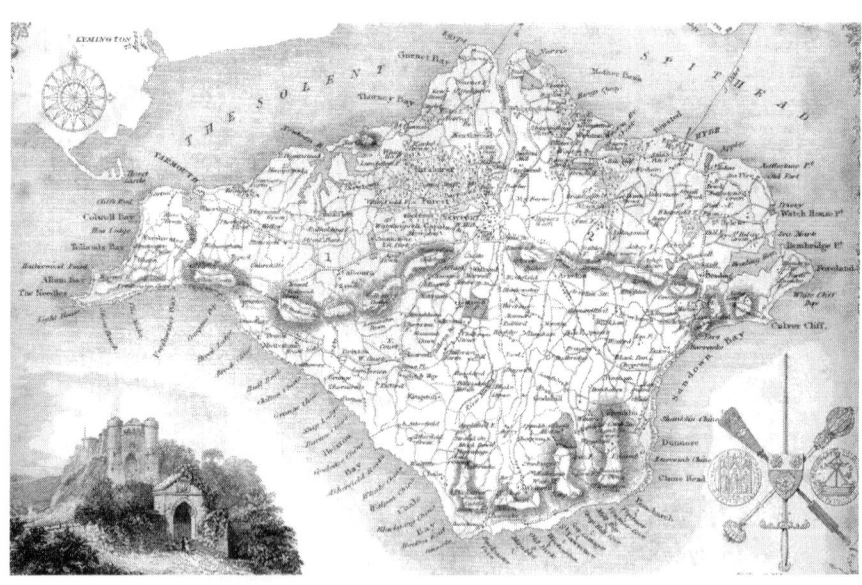

The Isle of Wight in the 1840s

The north east of the Island in 1883

The west of the Island in 1883

INTRODUCTION.

THE Isle of Wight (the Vecta or Vectis of the Romans) is separated from Hampshire, to which county it belongs, by an arm of the sea, called the Solent, the breadth of which varies from one to six miles. In this channel is the great harbour of Portsmouth and many other places of perfect security, where ships may ride at anchor. The best of these is Spithead, the great anchorage of the British fleet. The form of the island is an irregular ellipsis, measuring 23 miles from east to west, and 13 miles from north to south. Its circumference is about 60 miles, and its superficial contents 93,341 acres, of which a great portion is highly productive. It was formerly covered with woods, but it has been in a great measure denuded of these owing to its vicinity to Portsmouth, and the great demand of that naval arsenal for timber.

The face of the country may be described as undulating, rather than hilly, although there is a range of hills, or downs, running from east to west, through the island, with a few points of considerable elevation.* There is a great variety of rural scenery, adorned with a great diversity of foliage; and the island, especially the half of it north of the main range of downs, is even now, to a great extent, covered with woods and copses, while the fields are enclosed within hedge-rows, among which fine trees, and

* In the Geological Museum, Jermyn Street, London, are preserved the topographical and geological models of the Isle of Wight, constructed by the late Captain Ibbetson. They are very interesting, and most useful to the intending visitor.

especially stately elms, grow most luxuriantly; these, added to the beauty of the verdant fields and glimpses of the sea, present to the eye a succession of pleasing prospects. The two sides of the island possess each a peculiar character. The northern side is much wooded, whilst the southern, or the part called the *Back of the Island*, has far less timber, and the shores abound in bold rocks, precipitous projections, ravines, deep chasms, and other features of the imposing, and a few even of the sublime. In some parts these opposite characters are mingled. On the south side of the island there is a tract of land, known as the *Undercliff*, about 7 miles in length and from a half to a quarter of a mile in breadth. This singular district consists of a series of terraces, formed by fragments of rocks, chalk, and sandstone, which have been detached from the cliffs and hills above, and deposited upon a substratum of white marl. The whole of this *Undercliff* is completely sheltered from the north, north-west, and west winds by the range of lofty downs or hills of chalk or sandstone, which rise boldly from the upper termination of these terraces, on elevations varying from four to six and seven hundred feet in height. The two extremities of the range are indeed higher, as St. Boniface Down is 780 feet above the level of the sea, and St. Catherine's Hill on the west nearly 835 feet. The protection afforded by this natural barrier is greatly increased by the very singular and striking abruptness with which it terminates on its southern aspect. This, in many places, consists of the bare perpendicular rock of sandstone; in others of chalk, assuming its characteristic rounded form, covered with a fine turf and underwood.

The river Medina, which rises at the foot of St. Catherine's Down and falls into the Solent at Cowes, divides the island into two *hundreds* of nearly equal extent, called respectively East and West Medina, the former comprehending 14, the latter 16, parishes.

The population of the island at the last census of 1881 was 73,044, being an increase of 6825 during the preceding ten years. Previously to the passing of the Reform Bill of 1832, the boroughs of Newport, Newtown, and Yarmouth, returned each two members to Parliament, but Newtown and Yarmouth were then disfranchised, and one member returned for the Isle, and two for the borough of Newport. By the Reform Bill of 1867, Newport was deprived of one of its members. There is therefore now one member for the Isle of Wight, and one member for Newport.

The Isle of Wight was first invaded by the Romans A.D. 43, in the reign of the Emperor Claudius, and they retained possession of it till 530, when it was reduced by Cedric the Saxon. It suffered severely during the wars of the Saxon heptarchy, and was also frequently plundered and devastated by the Danes. It was on various occasions invaded by the French, but in almost every attack they were beaten and driven back to their ships by the islanders, who had made systematic preparations for their defence. After the naval superiority of England was established the island was further secured from the calamities of foreign invasion, and during the civil war between Charles I. and his Parliament, the inhabitants enjoyed comparative freedom from the prevailing commotions.

The Lordship of the island was conferred by William the Conqueror on William Fitz-Osborne, who is known in English history under the title of the Earl of Hereford, and for more than two centuries the island continued to be governed by its independent lords. But in 1293, Edward I. purchased the regalities for the sum of 6000 marks, an amount nearly approaching in purchasing power £60,000 of our money, from Isabella de Fortibus, Lady of Wight, and since that time the island has been governed by wardens, appointed by the Crown. The office has now become honorary, and, as is understood, unaccompanied by any salary.

King Henry VI. conferred the title of King of the Isle of Wight upon Henry Beauchamp, Duke of Warwick, and crowned him with his own hands; but the empty title expired with the nobleman who first bore it;—the Duke of Warwick dying in 1445.

The Isle of Wight derives additional interest from the fact of its having become a stated place of residence by her present Majesty, who, in 1844, conjointly with the late Prince Consort, purchased the mansion of Osborne, with its park, and the adjoining estate of Barton. Osborne House, the residence of Her Majesty, is situated in the immediate neighbourhood of East Cowes, and near the north coast of the island.

The principal towns and villages in the island are Ryde, Cowes, and Yarmouth upon the north coast ; Newport, with the adjacent village of Carisbrook, in the centre ; Ventnor and Bonchurch on the south ; Freshwater at the west end of the island ; and at the eastern end Shanklin, Sandown, and Bembridge.

RYDE.

Hotels: *Pier Hotel*, adjoining the Pier, table-d'hôte in the summer, 5s.; *Esplanade*, facing the sea; *Yelf's*, in Union Street; *Sivier's*, near the club; *York*, in George Street; *Kent*, commercial.
2d-Class Inns: *Eagle, Belgrave, Crown*.
House-agents: Wallis, Riddett, and Down; Marvin; and Scott.
Baths at the Victoria Pier.
Banks: National Provincial Bank of England, and the Capital and Counties Bank.
Railway to VENTNOR, *viâ* Brading, Sandown, Shanklin, and Wroxall; and to NEWPORT and COWES.
During the summer months Coaches and Chars-a-banc leave Ryde for Sandown, Shanklin, Newport, and Carisbrook, returning the same day.
[Ryde to Binstead, 1¼ m.; Quarr Abbey, 1¼ m.; Wootton Bridge, 1 m.; Newport, 3½ m. Total, Ryde to Newport, 7 miles.]

So large a majority of visitors to the Isle of Wight land at the town of Ryde, that we shall commence our explorations at this most popular watering-place.

Its appearance is eminently attractive, especially when seen from the water, which is here about four miles broad. The hill-side on which it clusters presents an amphitheatre of pleasant villas, set round with trim gardens and belts of vigorous trees; out of which springs the spire of TRINITY CHURCH on the left, the spire of the CONGREGATIONAL CHURCH in the centre, and the spires of ST. THOMAS' and ALL SAINTS' CHURCHES on the right. Leading up from the pier stretches the broad but somewhat precipitous UNION STREET, the principal thoroughfare of the town. To the right is BRIGSTOCKE TERRACE, and almost beneath it, the VICTORIA YACHT CLUB HOUSE shows

Edwardian tourists on Ryde Pier

its long line of windows and its saluting battery. Away to the west lies an undulating shore, well wooded in many parts, and broken into by sequestered creeks and abrupt coves,—the view terminating agreeably with the Italian campaniles of OSBORNE. To the east we see in succession the ESPLANADE, the Elizabethan turrets of APPLEY TOWERS standing on a commanding ascent, the point at SEA VIEW, and the wooded banks which contribute to the security of ST. HELEN'S ROADS.

The approach to Ryde is one of its principal "lions,"— presenting itself in the form of an admirable wooden PIER, whose extreme length is 2250 feet, and its breadth from 12 to 20 feet. It was commenced by a joint-stock company in 1813, and opened the following year, its length then being 1740 feet. In 1824 300 feet were added, and in 1833 it received a further addition. The pier-head and pavilion date from 1842. In 1856, and subsequently, further extensions took place; in 1860 a tramway was laid down alongside for the conveyance of passengers, and of heavy goods to and from the shipping. Whilst still more recently, an iron railway pier has been built by the South Western and South Coast Railway Companies, with a large railway station at the end, in order to bring the trains down alongside the steamboats. Another pier, "The Victoria," was commenced by a joint-stock company, but never completed, and is now used for baths.

The agreeable sanitary features of the town were recognised as early as the middle of the last century by the novelist Fielding, and as his remarks are still applicable, they may with propriety be quoted. "This pleasant village," he says, "is situated on a gentle ascent from the water, whence it affords that charming prospect I have already described. Its soil is a gravel, which, associated with its declivity, preserves it always so dry that immediately after the most violent rain a fine lady may walk without wetting her silken shoes. The fertility of the place is apparent from its extraordinary verdure; and it is so shaded with large and flourishing elms that its narrow lanes are a natural grove or walk, which in the regularity of its plantation vies with the power of art, and in its wanton exuberance greatly exceeds it."

The ESPLANADE, begun 1856-7, stretches along the sea-wall, and is nearly a mile in length. About 20 acres have been reclaimed from the sea, and laid out as public gardens, with an ornamental sheet of water. The latter is made of a uniform depth of about 18 inches, in order that children may paddle in it without danger. This artificial lake is a great attraction to children in the summer time, as it affords a safe and sheltered place for them to swim their boats; whilst in the winter it forms an admirable sheet of ice for skaters.

The PUBLIC BUILDINGS of the town are few and unimportant. The most striking is the TOWN HALL and MARKET HOUSE in Lind Street, first erected in 1829-31, from the designs of an architect named Sanderson, and at an expense of £5000. It has since been greatly added to. The centre exhibits an Ionic portico, supported by a Doric colonnade, over which is a lofty tower containing a clock and chimes. The market in the left wing is little used. The right wing is devoted to various offices. The TOWN HALL contains several very fine rooms, one capable of holding nearly 1000 people; the Council Chamber; Police Court; and the usual Municipal Offices.

Westward of the pier stands the CLUB HOUSE of the ROYAL VICTORIA YACHT CLUB—a large building with a saluting battery, whose first stone was laid by the Prince Consort in 1846. It was, in 1864, enlarged and much improved by the addition of a new Italian façade with ornamental pillars, etc. The CLUB itself was established May 24, 1845, and enrols about 150 yachts, with an aggregate tonnage of 8000 tons. Entrance-fee, £5 : 5s.; yearly subscription, £5 : 5s. The regatta is held about the second week in August, and is followed, a week or two later, by a town regatta.

In UNION STREET the visitor will observe a covered promenade, bordered by shops, and terminating in a semicircular vestibule, which bears the loyal appellation of the ROYAL VICTORIA ARCADE. It was built in 1835, from the designs of Westmacott, at the cost of £10,000.

The present THEATRE, a very well-arranged house, replaces the old theatre (built in 1816), at the top of Union Street. During the season a succession of London companies add to the attractions of the town.

The INFIRMARY is a commodious edifice, situate at the top of the High Street; it has accommodation for fifty patients.

The CHURCHES are well worth visiting. The parish of Ryde was formed in 1866 by a special Act of Parliament, by which the advowson of Newchurch (also constituted a separate parish) was directed to be sold, and the proceeds (£3500) applied to the building of a new parish church. This sum has been largely increased by private subscriptions, and a very fine church, dedicated to ALL SAINTS (costing over £20,000), has been erected, in the Decorated style, after designs by the late Sir Gilbert Scott. The reredos, pulpit, and font, are elaborate works of art, of variously-coloured marbles; and there is much good painted glass, the west window of the nave being particularly fine. At the east end of the north aisle is a magnificent tower and spire nearly 200 feet high, visible for many miles in every direction. Visitors should ascend the tower, for which a small charge is made.

ST. THOMAS' CHURCH, in St. Thomas' Street, is a poor building, possessing no interest. It is covered on the outside with ivy, which, to a certain extent, gives it a picturesque appearance. At the west end is a tower and spire.

ST. JAMES' CHURCH, in Lind Street, is an ugly building, choked up with pews and galleries. It is the "Evangelical" Church of Ryde.

St. MARY'S CATHOLIC CHURCH, in the High Street, was erected in 1845, at the sole cost of the late Countess of Clare. It has a low tower containing four bells. There is some good painted glass, and a rather fine painting of the Crucifixion over the high altar.

TRINITY CHURCH, in Dover Street, is a large church, with a lofty tower and spire. There is a great deal of painted glass, most of it very bad.

St. Michael and All Angels is a cruciform church, with a central tower, containing three bells. It was erected from the designs of Mr. R. J. Cornewall Jones, M.R.I.B.A. There is a good deal of fine painted glass, and over the altar is a very fair tryptych. The services at this church are of the most advanced ritualistic type.

St. John's Church is another cruciform church, with a good deal of fair glass in it.

The Independent Chapel, in George Street, is a large edifice in the Gothic style. It was erected in 1870 from the designs of Mr. R. J. Cornewall Jones. The new Baptist Chapel, in the same street, is a neat building, with a thin spire.

The Cemetery, consecrated in 1842, and enlarged in 1862, and still more recently in 1881, is situate in West Street.

The Government School of Art, in George Street, is a large building, with numerous class-rooms and a small Museum.

The Isle of Wight College, a public school for the sons of gentlemen, is at the east end of the town.

The Young Men's Christian Association, in Lind Street, has a library and public reading-rooms.

The Conservative Club, in the High Street, is a very good working-men's club, fitted up with reading, smoking, and billiard-rooms.

It is interesting to notice the rapid growth of Ryde. In the reign of Richard II. it was burnt by the French as one of those places where "watch and ward" were kept in those troublous times for the defence of the island, and up to the commencement of the present century it was nothing but a collection of fishermen's huts on the shore, and a few straggling cottages on the crest of the hill. It was then divided into Lower and Upper Ryde, and separated by a leafy screen of trees. It received a charter of incorporation in 1868, and has now a population of 15,000.

Our route from Ryde to Newport (the capital of the island) traverses a very agreeable and well-wooded country.

"Its charms arise," says an Edinburgh Reviewer, "from the sight of verdure and fertility spread over an undulating and well-wooded surface, many points commanding fine views of the sea, and particularly of the strait which separates the island from the coast of England." We advise the tourist to turn aside, however, from the main road, and cross the fields as far as Wootton Bridge.

Quitting Ryde, therefore, by the Spencer Road (observe on the right, WESTFIELD, the seat of Sir Robert Clifford; and Ryde House, the seat of Sir Henry Daly), we turn off to the north-west by a footpath up hill and down hill, through pleasant meadows and green hedgerows, and crossing the tiny brook which separates the parish of Ryde from that of Binstead, climb the ascent, which is crowned by BINSTEAD CHURCH ($1\frac{1}{4}$ mile). The quarries in this vicinity produced a species of limestone composed of comminuted shells held together by sparry calcareous cement, which yielded a stone sufficiently firm for building purposes. This stone was largely employed by Bishops Walkelyn and William of Wykeham, in the erection of Winchester Cathedral. Fresh-water shells abound here, and teeth and bones of mammalia, seed-vessels and stems of aquatic plants, often repay the geologist's well-directed inquiries. The quarries are now, however, extinct.

The CHURCH, dedicated to the Holy Cross, was rebuilt in 1842, from the designs of Mr. T. Hellyer. What was once the old Norman north door of the church has been barbarously set up as a gateway into the churchyard. Over the door is a curious old Norman figure.

In the rear of the church, surrounded by beautiful grassy slopes, stands a villa, lately the residence of the Queen's Physician, Sir Charles Locock; and, in a delightful breadth of blooming garden, on the left, is the picturesque rectory-house.

Passing the church we enter, on the right hand, a long stretch of low oak copses, commanding at several points views of Spithead and the blue line of the Hampshire coast beyond. In the hollow to which we now descend lie the scanty remains of the once famous.

QUARR ABBEY, anciently Quarraria, from the quarries in its neighbourhood. Out of its ruins have been constructed a deformed farm-house and its appendant buildings, and a large barn, whose walls are ancient, and which was, it is said, the monastic refectory. Remark a small building (to the east) with a Perpendicular door, and three arches in tolerable preservation; remains of a fine Decorated doorway, a moulded segmental arch, and a few other remains of the old work may also be seen. Quarr Abbey was founded in 1132 by Baldwin de Redvers, afterwards Lord of the Island and Earl of Devon. He planted here a small colony of monks from the Benedictine abbey of Savigny in Normandy, which, in 1148, was attached to the Cistercian order. Quarr thus became the second Cistercian house established in England. It was dedicated by its founder to the Virgin Mary, and amply endowed with lands—an example which his successors imitated, so that, in due time, the Abbot of Quarr became one of the leading magnates of the island. By license from Edward III., the abbey, which was often exposed to the attacks of French sea-rovers, was fortified with a stone wall enclosing an area of 40 acres. The sea-gate and considerable portions of the wall may still be traced.

Many distinguished personages were buried at Quarr:—the founder, and his wife Adeliza; William de Vernon, lord of the island, who bequeathed £300 for the erection of a stately monument; and the Lady Cicely, second daughter of Edward IV., whose life, in its changes and contrasts, might well attract the attention of the romancist.

At the suppression of religious houses, the yearly revenue of Quarr was £181 : 15 : 2. In 1404 it was computed at £96 : 13 : 4. The abbey was purchased, and rudely demolished, by a Mr. Mills of Southampton, whose son's widow, Mrs. Dowsabell Mills, became the mistress of Sir Edward Horsey, captain of the island. Sir Thomas Fleming, Lord Chief-Justice, *temp.* James I., purchased the manor of her representatives, and in the Fleming family it still remains.

Among the numerous traditions attached to Quarr and its vicinity, there is one that connects a wood now consisting of brushwood and a few decayed oaks, called Eleanor's Grove, with the queen of Henry II., who was said to have been imprisoned at Quarr, and to have loved to wander in this secluded spot.

Continuing our ramble we soon arrive at FISHBOURNE, a small collection of houses at the mouth of Fishbourne Creek, or, as it is more commonly called, WOOTTON RIVER. At high water—for the river is tidal as far as Wootton Bridge—the scene from this point is by no means devoid of beauty. The sloping banks are fringed with oak-copses, whose pendent branches are pleasantly reflected in the waves beneath; which, above the village of Wootton, broaden into a fair-sized lake.

The high road from Ryde to Newport crosses the creek at WOOTTON BRIDGE. (*The Sloop*, a small public-house.) A new bridge has been lately constructed here, and the approaches, which were awkward, have been very much improved. Crossing the bridge we ascend a steep hill, upon whose declivity clusters the little village of Wootton. On our left, a high tower, rising above the richly-wooded uplands, belongs to FERN HILL, a house of some pretensions, built (1791-1795) by the Right Hon. Thomas Orde, afterwards Lord Bolton, during his governorship of the island. Ascending the hill we arrive at the picturesque OLD RECTORY, where are preserved some interesting relics of Izaak Walton, to whose family the late rector belonged.

☞ At this point two roads branch off from our main route; that to the right leads, across green meadows, to WOOTTON CHURCH, and thence, through Barton, to East Cowes. The left road conducts us to ARRETON.

☞ WOOTTON CHURCH, a long narrow edifice, consisting of a nave and chancel, was built by one of the De Insulas, or L'Isles, a famous old island family, long time lords of Wootton. It is dedicated to St. Edmund. Its points of interest are—a Norman doorway, with chevron mouldings, on the south; an Early English arch, which formerly opened into the chantry of St. Edmund the King; and the Early Decorated windows on the east and west. Observe the pulpit, *temp.* James I., and the memorial to Sir *William*

Lisle, d. 1665. Sir William, by the way, was the royalist brother of the regicide, Sir *John Lisle*, one of Cromwell's peers, and a sturdy Puritan, slain at Lausanne, after the Restoration, by two Irish bravoes. His widow, Dame *Alice Lisle*, was condemned to death by Judge Jeffreys (A.D. 1686) for having mercifully sheltered two fugitives from the fatal field of Sedgemoor.

We now turn aside for a while from our Newport route, to examine the road to Arreton (3 miles).

Branch Route—Wootton to Arreton.

On our right lie a succession of copses, affording pleasant effects of light and shadow; on our left extend the grounds of Fernhill. Passing these we turn aside to the left, and adopt a road which is agreeably picturesque, winding through deep banks clothed with verdure, with trailing ivy, and ferns, and grasses, and wild flowers. Crossing Arreton Down, from the top of which a magnificent panorama of the interior of the island is obtained, we descend into the valley of Arreton (population 2140; upon the summit of the down is a poor little public-house called *The Hare and Hounds*), one of the fairest spots in the Isle of Wight. Its Church stands upon a slight ascent which rises gently from the road—a fine old building, containing traces of all the different styles of Gothic, from the Norman of the eleventh century to the Perpendicular of the sixteenth. The windows of the chancel are extremely good specimens of very Early Decorated work of about 1300. Observe the aumbry in the north wall of the chancel; and the remarkable brass in the south chancel, date 1430, exhibiting the effigy of an armed knight, and an epitaph in black letter—

> Here is y buried vnder this graue
> Harry Hawles his soul God saue
> Longe tyme steward of ye yle of Wyght
> Have mercy on hym God ful of myght.

A brass plate against a pillar in the south aisle commemorates, in uncouth rhymes, the good deeds of one *William*

Serle, d. 1595. There are several memorials to members of the Holmes family—especially that by Westmacott to *Richard Fleming Worsley*—and the churchyard is unusually full of noticeable inscriptions. One of the most interesting of these is to the memory of *Elizabeth Wallbridge*, the "Dairyman's Daughter," whose simple story was told so effectively by the Rev. Legh Richmond.*

Just beyond the church stands the ancient MANOR HOUSE, *temp.* James I., now occupied as a farm. The interior contains some excellent carving. From here the tourist may ascend the ridge of chalk-hills, on which are several barrows of Anglo-Saxon date, and turning to the left, as if to cross ST. GEORGE'S DOWN, descend to the manor-house of EAST STANDEN, noticeable from its historical associations. The present building is of Georgian date, but occupies the site of the ancient residence of the Lady Cicely, second daughter of Edward IV., and a woman of singular beauty and merit. She stooped from her high estate, soon after her sister Elizabeth's marriage to Henry VII., to ally herself with John, Lord Wells, a gallant soldier, about twice her own age. Left a widow in 1498, she chose for her second husband a man of still lower degree, one Thomas Kyme, of the Kymes of Lincolnshire, with whom she retired (*circa* 1504) to the Isle of Wight, and by whom she is said to have had two children, Richard and Margerie. In the tranquillity of East Standen she spent three quiet years. Her death took place on the 24th of August 1507, in the 38th year of her age. She was buried at Quarr Abbey, and commemorated by a stately monument.

South-east of Arreton is Haseley, where, during his captaincy of the island, resided the bold and unscrupulous Sir Edward Horsey. He died here of the plague, in 1582.

[☞ From Arreton a glorious walk along the crest of the chalk ridge—Arreton, Ashey, and Brading Downs—may be extended to the village of BRADING, on the Ryde and Ventnor road. Or the tourist may stroll across St. George's Down to Shide, and thence to CARISBROOK or NEWPORT. A

---

* The epitaph is from the pen of the late Mrs. W. C. Bousfield, well known as a poetess among her own friends.

ramble of scarcely inferior interest may be made by way of Horringford, across the Yar or Main river, and passing the "DAIRYMAN'S DAUGHTER'S" COTTAGE, to SANDOWN, and its beautiful Bay; or the traveller may proceed from Arreton *viâ* Merston, to GODSHILL, and thence, through Whitwell, to St. Lawrence and the Undercliff.

In this neighbourhood the botanist may search for the *Verbascum nigrum, Anthemis arvensis*, and *Daphne laureola*. The high banks which shelter its "green and leafy lanes" are luxuriantly prodigal of clematis, woodbine, and polypody.]

MAIN ROUTE RESUMED—WOOTTON TO NEWPORT.

The country between Wootton and Newport is of a pleasing character, but scarcely calls for detailed description. The road crosses Wootton Heath; traverses the head of the small creek known as KING'S QUAY, from an old but erroneous tradition that its wooded shores afforded shelter to King John after his escape from the potent barons who had compelled his signature to Magna Charta; passes, on the right, the red brick buildings of the late Prince Consort's Farm, and after descending into the valley of the Medina, leaves behind it the respectable old mansion of FAIRLEE, and the recently constructed NEWPORT CEMETERY. Then it crosses the Medina at Coppin's Bridge, and connects itself with High Street, the main thoroughfare of Newport.

NEWPORT.

Hotels: *The Bugle*, in the High Street; *Warburton's*.
Inns: *The Star, Green Dragon, Wheatsheaf,* etc.
Banks: London and County, National Provincial, and Capital and Counties Bank. Population, 9430.
☞ CENTRAL STATION, from which trains run to Cowes, Ryde direct, Ryde *viâ* Sandown and Ventnor. FOUR-HORSE COACHES run in connection with the trains to Freshwater. There is also an OMNIBUS to Yarmouth.
A CARGO-BOAT leaves Newport Quay for West Cowes every tide.
Market-Day, Saturday. Cattle market every alternate Wednesday.

Newport is believed to be of Roman foundation, and numerous relics of the imperial colonists have been discovered here. The plan of the town as it is was laid out by Richard de Redvers, Earl of Devon and Lord of the Island, early in the reign of Henry I. "apportionments being let off for building at one shilling 'a place'" (*Venables*). From Richard de Redvers, third of the name, the rising town received its first charter ; and the privileges then granted were confirmed and enlarged by the famous Lady of the Island, Isabella de Fortibus. Fifteen charters, in amplification of these original provisions, were successively granted by our Sovereigns, from Richard II. to Charles II. Newport received its Charter of Incorporation in the year 1603, its governing body being a mayor, twenty-four councillors, a recorder, and a town-clerk. This arrangement was modified after the Restoration, and a mayor, eleven aldermen, and an equal number of burgesses, appointed. By the Municipal Corporation Act (William IV.) the corporation was again re-constituted, and now consists of a mayor, six aldermen, and eighteen town-councillors—the latter of whom are elected by the inhabitants.

In August 1377 the prosperity of the town was seriously checked by a French invasion. The ravages of the marauders were so destructive that for two years "no tenant was resident in the town," and a couple of centuries passed before it rose to any degree of wealth or importance. In 1582 its inhabitants were almost decimated by the plague. "The road to Carisbrook (the mother-church) was blocked up by the dead-carts, and so crowded was the cemetery that licence was accorded to the inhabitants to form a graveyard round their own church." But from this period the unfortunate town appears to have struggled into prosperity. A Town Hall and a Gaol were built, and an ordinary established, at which Sir John Oglander—an island-worthy, whose MSS. are full of curious details—had known "twelve knights and as many gentleman to attend." Camden speaks of it as being, in his time, "a toune well-seated and much frequented, populous with inhabitants, having an entrance into the isle from the haven and a passage for vessels of small burden unto the key."

Newport became, in 1648, the stage whereon was played out one of the most remarkable scenes in the terrible drama of the Civil War. It had previously been disturbed from its propriety by a silly attempt of Captain Burley, a royalist gentleman of Yarmouth, to provoke a re-action on behalf of Charles I. The outbreak was quickly put down by a detachment of soldiers from Carisbrook, and Captain Burley was seized, tried at Winchester for high treason, and executed on the 2d of February. The attachment of the majority of the inhabitants to the cause of the Parliament was not, however, to be questioned; and Newport was accordingly selected as the most convenient place for the negotiations commenced between the king and his opponents on Monday, 2d October 1648. These negotiations took place in the Grammar School, the king being seated in a chair of state under a canopy; on either side of a long table were ranged the Commissioners; behind the king stood his attendants, Sir P. Warwick, Sir Edward Walker, and others. The proceedings continued for sixty days. The king occupied the house of a private citizen, his attendants being accommodated at the George Inn on the south side of High Street (now destroyed), and the Commissioners staying at the Bull (now the Bugle) Inn.

Newport has been represented in Parliament by several historic worthies: Lord Falkland in 1640; Admiral Sir Robert Holmes in 1678-89; Lord Cutts, one of Marlborough's soldiers, 1698; Lord Palmerston in 1807; and the Right Honourable George Canning in 1826. Here were born the learned antiquarian divine, *Thomas James*, in 1571; his nephew, an erudite controversialist, *Richard James;* and Sir *Thomas Fleming*, who rose from a low estate to the dignity of Lord Chief-Justice of England, *temp.* James I.

The first point of interest to which the visitor should direct his steps is the CHURCH dedicated to St. Thomas of Canterbury, and erected, 1854-7, at a cost of over £12,000, from the designs of Mr. Daukes. This church replaced the old church dating from 1175, when it was erected by Richard de Redvers, and dedicated to the recently canonised Archbishop of Canterbury, Thomas à Becket. The memorials it contained are preserved in the present building—an Early Decorated structure of some size. The tower at the west end contains the fine peal of bells from the old church. The nave is clerestoried, and there are gabled aisles and a chancel. The PULPIT (from the old church) dates from 1633. Its carvings were the work of one Thomas Caper, whose device—a goat, in allusion to his name—may be seen on its back. Justice and Mercy figure on the sounding-board, around which is a sentence from the Psalms, " Cry aloud, and spare not : lift up thy voice like a trumpet." On the sides are sculptured a curious personification of the Three Graces, the Four Cardinal Virtues, and the Seven Liberal Sciences—grammar, dialectics, rhetoric, music, arithmetic, geometry, astrology. There is a monument to Sir *Edward Horsey*, formerly captain of the island (1565-82), representing his effigy, clad in armour, beneath a rich painted and gilded canopy, and an epitaph, which ascribes to him many more virtues than we fear he possessed. The memorial (by Marochetti) erected by the queen to Charles I.'s ill-fated daughter, the *Princess Elizabeth*, represents her as, according to tradition, she was discovered by her attendants, reclining in death upon her couch, her hands folded in prayer, and her face resting on the pages of an open Bible, a gift from her royal father. Her body was buried in the chancel of the Old Church on the 20th of September 1650, but its resting-place was totally forgotten until, in 1793, some labourers, engaged in digging a grave for the Honourable Septimus West, discovered the royal maiden's coffin. The place of interment was then indicated by a stone bearing a suitable inscription.

There is a good deal of very bad painted glass in the church, and in the north aisle is a medallion likeness, in white marble, of the late Prince Albert.

The CHURCH OF ST. JOHN, at Node Hill, on the road to Shide, is a building of no architectural pretension. It was erected in 1837 at the cost of about £4500. At Barton village, on the east side of the town, is ST. PAUL'S CHURCH, also of no merit architecturally, erected in 1844 at the cost of about £2000. ST. THOMAS' CATHOLIC CHURCH is in Pyle

Street. It is an ugly red-brick building, utterly devoid of interest.

The Independents have a chapel in St. James' Street, erected, in 1848, on the site of a chapel first erected in 1699, and rebuilt in 1777. There is another Independent Chapel at Node Hill, and a Baptist Chapel in Castlehold.

The GRAMMAR SCHOOL, founded in 1612 by Lord Chief-Justice Fleming, is a noticeable Jacobean mansion. The schoolroom remains in nearly the same condition as when it was occupied by Charles I. during the negotiations which resulted in the abortive treaty of Newport. It was here the unfortunate monarch was seized by Major Rolph and his myrmidons, November 30, 1648, and from hence he was hurried to Hurst Castle.

The TOWN HALL, from the designs of Nash, a plain structure, with an Ionic portico and colonnade, was built in 1816. The lower portion is used as a market-house, whilst above is the Council-Chamber and Police Court.

The ISLE OF WIGHT LITERARY INSTITUTION is situate at the corner of High Street and St. James' Square, it was erected in 1810 at the cost of about £3000. It has an extensive library, and a well supplied news-room. The annual subscription is £2 : 2s. The ISLE OF WIGHT MUSEUM, at the corner of St. James' Street and Crocker Street, contains a small collection of antiquities, fossils, etc., connected with the island. In Lugley Street is THE BLUE SCHOOL, established in 1761, for educating and clothing poor girls. In St. Thomas' Square, opposite the principal entrance to the church, is the Corn Exchange.

Small vessels come up the river with the tide as far as Newport, and the number of warehouses in the neighbourhood of its small quay show that in this way a considerable trade is carried on. It is also the centre of a considerable trade with the surrounding country.

About 2 miles below the town, on the west bank of the river, are the extensive cement works of Messrs. Francis Brothers and Co. of Nine Elms, London, who employ here about 100 hands in the manufacture of Portland and Medina cements. There are several nurseries about the town.

The position of Newport, in a valley watered by the Medina, and sheltered by the downs, cannot but commend itself to the visitor's attention.

> " Set in the midst of our meridian Isle,
> By wandering heaths and pensive woods embraced,
> With dewy meads, and downs of open smile,
> And winding waters, naturally graced,
> The rural capital is meetly placed.
> Newport, so long as to the blue-eyed deep
> Thy river by its gleamy wings is traced,
> Be it thine thy portion unimpaired to keep !"—*Edmund Peel.*

The neighbourhood abounds in pleasant rambles, and the Branch Routes we are about to indicate will conduct the traveller into a number of agreeable landscapes.

NEWPORT to PARKHURST FOREST.

We leave Newport by St. James' Street, cross one branch of the Medina, and passing the site of the ancient priory of Holy Cross, commence our ascent of Honey or Hunny Hill. The HOUSE OF INDUSTRY, established by Act of Parliament in 1770 for "the maintenance and employment of the poor of the Isle of Wight, by a general consolidation of the poor-rates"— the prototype, in fact, of the new poor law system—is now conspicuous on our right. We next arrive at the ALBANY BARRACKS, named after the Duke of York and Albany, Commander-in-chief, and erected in 1798, now always called " Parkhurst." The parade-ground is of great extent, and the barracks themselves are capable of accommodating between 2000 or 3000 soldiers.

Just beyond stands the PARKHURST PRISON, which was established in 1838 as a " General Penitentiary for Juvenile Offenders ;" but owing to the establishment of reformatories in various parts, it came to be less required for its original purpose, and the juveniles have been removed. At present the building is used as a general prison for convicts.

Away to the westward spreads PARKHURST FOREST—a "cantle" of the old royal Park of Watchingwell, the first royal chase established in England[*]— still retaining the

[*] It is mentioned in Domesday Book as the King's Park, and extended from the Medina to Newtown River, east to west, and from the Solent to the Chalk Downs, north to south.

appellation of "Forest," though its primeval grandeur has entirely disappeared, and it now mainly consists of large plantations of stunted oaks and young firs. It offers, nevertheless, many pleasant walks ; many rambles under green leaves, and through shady glades.

COWES AND NEWPORT RAILWAY.

This line of railway now connects the towns of Cowes and Newport. About midway is NORTHWOOD (population in 1881, 8175, including West Cowes), whose CHURCH, dedicated to St. John the Baptist, remained a chapelry to Carisbrook, until the reign of Henry VIII. Its general characteristics are Transition-Norman, and the south door is Norman, with a zig-zag moulding. In 1856 it was repaired by a local builder, and nearly all its features of interest were destroyed.

WEST COWES.

Hotels: *The Gloster* (the best); *The Fountain*, close to the pier, good; *Marine*, on the Parade ; *Vine*, and many smaller Inns. Population 6077.

From the erection of a small castle by King Henry in 1540, whose materials were obtained out of the ruins of the famous Abbey of Beaulieu, dates the history of WEST COWES, though its growth was slow, and even in Charles I.'s time it contained but half a dozen houses. The advantages afforded by its commodious harbour became, however, gradually appreciated, and Sir John Oglander tells us that in 1620 he had seen 300 ships there at anchor.

The world-famous YACHT-BUILDING YARDS of the Messrs. White were originated in 1815. The MEDINA DOCK was built in 1845 ; it is 330 feet long by 62 feet wide. The vessels launched by this enterprising firm are celebrated for their sea-going qualities. But long before Messrs. White's time, Cowes was celebrated for its dockyards. Nelson's ship the Vanguard, the Repulse, of sixty-four guns ; the Salisbury, fifty ; the Cerberus, thirty-two ; the Veteran, sixty-four; and many other line of battle ship's were built at Cowes.

As a watering-place the popularity of West Cowes dates from the establishment of the ROYAL YACHT CLUB in 1812, and the foundation of a Club House in 1815. But its facilities for sea-bathing were appreciated at an earlier period. A rhymester, named Henry Jones, in a poem dedicated to the glorification of the Isle of Wight, and published in 1760, exclaims—

"No more to foreign baths shall Britain roam,
But plunge at Cowes, and find rich health at home."

The ROYAL YACHT SQUADRON includes about 300 members, and registers about 150 yachts, which employ upwards of 2000 seamen, and presents a total of upwards of 15,000 tons. Each member has a warrant from the Admiralty to carry the St. George's ensign, and the yachts are admitted into foreign ports free of port-dues. The yachting season lasts from May to October. The Regatta takes place annually in August, and is under the immediate patronage of Royalty. His Royal Highness the Prince of Wales is the Commodore. Entrance-fee, £15; annual subscription, £8.

The CASTLE was purchased by the Club in 1856 as the Club House, and has been refitted and repaired at a considerable expense. For a long period it had simply served as a pleasant residence for a sinecure Governor. During the Commonwealth and Protectorate it was chiefly made use of as a state prison, and here Sir William Davenant, during his incarceration, wrote a portion of his epic of *Gondibert*. A small garrison occupied it during the Revolutionary War.

The ROYAL LANDINGS at Cowes have been numerous. Henry VIII. disembarked here in 1538, and proceeded to Appuldurcombe, on a visit to his favourite Richard Worsley, Captain of the Island. On August 2, 1609, it was visited by James I. and Prince Charles, on their way to enjoy the pleasures of the chase in Parkhurst Forest; and on the 27th August 1618, by Prince Charles alone, who afterwards patronised with his presence a military display. Charles I.

landed here, September 22, 1647, as a prisoner, on his way to Carisbrook ; and his children, the Princess Elizabeth and the young Duke of Gloucester, on Tuesday, August 13, 1650. The Duke of York, afterwards James II., was here in 1673.

Morland, the artist, resided at West Cowes for some months, in 1799. Sir Charles Fellowes, the Lycian traveller, was also one of its more distinguished residents until his death. He erected the row of houses known as THE TERRACE on the Marine Parade, and was unceasingly active in promoting the prosperity of the town.

Beyond the Castle, and extending along the shore of the Solent, is THE GREEN, which was laid out and presented to the inhabitants by G. R. Stephenson, Esq., and forms an agreeable promenade.

The Old CHURCH of West Cowes (a chapelry of Northwood and a perpetual curacy in the gift of the Vicar of Carisbrook) was built in 1653, and is one of the four churches built in this country during the usurpation of Oliver Cromwell. It was consecrated upon the Restoration of Charles II. in 1661, by Morley, bishop of Winchester. In 1811, it was enlarged, at the cost of George Ward, Esq. of Northwood Park, from the designs of Nash, by whom the tower was added as a mausoleum for the Ward family. The old church was pulled down and was replaced by the present church, the foundation-stone of which was laid 2d May 1867, and it was opened on 28th May 1868. HOLY TRINITY CHURCH, at the back of the Castle, was founded in 1832 by Mrs. Goodwin. It is a large ugly building. At the east end is a new chancel built from the designs of Mr. R. J. Cornewall Jones. The Roman Catholic Church of St. Thomas of Canterbury is situate in Carvel Lane. It possesses no features of interest. The NATIONAL SCHOOLS were erected in 1821, on ground presented by the late Mr. Ward. The Dissenters possess various places of worship —the *Independents*, in Union Road, the *Wesleyans*, in Birmingham Road.

Above the town, on the crest of the hill, stands the house called NORTHWOOD PARK, the seat of W. G. Ward, Esq., the lord of the manor.

A pleasant walk along the MARINE PARADE leads to the point called EGYPT. From this point may be enjoyed a surprisingly beautiful prospect of the Hampshire coast, Eaglehurst and Calshot Castle, and the waters of the Solent. The ramble may be continued to GURNET BAY, where Charles II. landed in 1671 on his way to Yarmouth. The tin-trade is supposed by some authorities to have been carried on between a port which formerly existed here and LEAP, on the opposite shore. The low cliffs in the vicinity of THORNESS BAY consist of Bembridge limestone, and a few fossils may occasionally be obtained. The tourist may here ascend from the shore by Whippence Farm into the road, and return to West Cowes by Tinker's Lane through Lower Cockleton.

The return to Newport may be varied by turning to the right past Northwood Church to the river bank at WERROR FARM, crossing the Medina to the FOLLY INN (noted for its oysters). Ascending into the East Cowes road, and so into Newport by Fairlee.

NEWPORT TO OSBORNE AND EAST COWES.

The principal points of interest in this short but agreeable route (5 miles) are quickly enumerated. FAIRLEE is an old and unpretending mansion, formerly occupied by a branch of the ancient Oglander family, and pleasantly situated on the uplands, above the winding river. The neat cottages erected by Her Majesty and the late Prince Consort on their estates, and the late Prince Consort's farm-buildings, are seen on our right. From various points we command very good views of the river and valley of the Medina.

A road on the left descends the hill-side to WHIPPINGHAM (population, 4578), a parish which includes in its area of 4638 acres East Cowes and a considerable portion of the Osborne estate. THE CHURCH was rebuilt in 1860 by Mr. A. J. Humbert, under the direction of the late Prince Consort, who took a special interest in the work. It is a cruciform structure, of a kind of German Romanesque in style, with an aisled chancel, and large central tower surmounted by a spire. The Church is seated with low, open seats, and in the chancel is a white marble monument, by Theed, to the late Prince, erected by Her Majesty. Two angels are represented holding an *immortelle* wreath, and crowning a medallion bust of the Prince. The monument records that it "is placed in the Church, erected under his direction, by his broken-hearted widow, Queen Victoria. 1864." In the interior is also a plain memorial to Dr. Arnold's father. The Royal Family, who, when at Osborne, usually attend this church, occupy the south chancel aisle, so that they can see the clergyman at the reading desk and the altar without themselves being seen by the general public in the nave. The Royal household occupy the other chancel aisle.

A pretty rural lane now runs parallel for about three-quarters of a mile with the East Cowes road, and eventually joins it near to one of the principal entrances of

OSBORNE.

This royal manor was anciently called Austerbourne or Oysterbourne, and derives its name, it is said, from the "oyster-beds of the Medina." From the Bowermans, an old island-family not yet extinct, the estate passed into the hands of one Eustace Mann, who, during the troubles of the Civil War, buried a mass of gold and silver coins in a coppice still known as *Money Coppice*, and having forgotten to mark the spot, was never afterwards able to recover his treasure. A Mr. Blachford married his granddaughter, and transmitted the estate to his heirs. From Lady Isabella Blachford it was purchased by Her Majesty in 1840, and it has since been enlarged by the addition of Barton and other demesnes, until it includes an area of upwards of 5000 acres,—bounded, north by the Solent, south by the Ryde and Newport road, east by the inlet of King's Quay, and west by the Medina. The stone mansion, built by Mr.

Blachford, was pulled down when the Queen became its possessor, and the present Palace of Osborne erected, in the Italian style, under the direction of Mr. T. Cubitt. The campanile is 90 feet high, the flag-tower 112. The royal apartments are adorned by a large and choice collection of statuary and paintings, and look out upon terraced gardens, and a breadth of lawn which stretches to the shore of the Solent. The surrounding grounds are of considerable beauty, and the farm is benefited by the introduction of every modern improvement. The best view of Osborne is obtained from the water. Neither the house nor grounds are opened to the public.

The manor of BARTON, or BURTON, lies to the east. An Oratory was founded here in 1272 by John de Insula and Peter de Winton, respectively the rectors of Shalfleet and Godshill, for the reception of an arch-priest, six chaplains, and a clerk, of the Augustinian order. Its lands were granted in the fifteenth century to Winchester College; from whose authorities they were purchased by Her Majesty. The head steward of the royal estates resides in BARTON COURT HOUSE, recently rebuilt, but still retaining its characteristic Tudor front.

The road skirts the Osborne estate for a considerable distance. Near the principal entrance, and adjoining the road which descends through EAST COWES PARK (an unfortunate building speculation) to East Cowes, stands the gateway of EAST COWES CASTLE (Lord Gort), erected by Nash, George IV.'s architect, for his own residence. The grounds are admirably arranged. A noble conservatory, 250 feet long, is a splendid adjunct. The picture gallery and library are richly fitted up.

Lower down the hill, on the right, is SLATWOODS (the residence of Captain Simmonds), which the tourist will regard with more than ordinary interest as the birthplace of the great and good Dr. Arnold (June 13, 1795). His father was collector of customs at East Cowes, and died here in 1801. The great historian and educational reformer never forgot the scene of his earlier days, and from the large willow-tree—still remaining in the grounds—

transplanted slips successively to Laleham, Rugby, and Fox How.—(*Dean Stanley's Life and Letters of Arnold.*)

A private road, passing SPRING HILL (Mrs. Shedden), ascends to NORRIS CASTLE (His Grace, the Duke of Bedford), a noble castellated mansion, built for Lord Henry Seymour by Sir J. Wyattville. Its ivy-covered front is bold and picturesque; and the glorious prospects which it commands of Southampton Water, and the spires and masts beyond— of the distant hills of the New Forest—and the wooded coast of the island as far as St. Helen's, are eminently striking in their constantly varying effects of light and shade.

George IV. was received here by Lord Henry Seymour in 1819, and it was a favourite residence of Her Majesty, while Princess Victoria. The Duchess of Kent occupied it in the summer of 1859, and in 1881 the Crown Prince and Princess of Germany.

Retracing our steps, we turn at once into the village of EAST COWES (Inn: *The East Medina*), where it will be unnecessary to detain the tourist for any lengthened period. Of East Cowes Castle, which Henry VIII. constructed upon the ruins of a cell attached to the abbey of Beaulieu, and known as EAST SHAMBLORD, there are no remains; but its position is still known as OLD CASTLE POINT. (Shamblord, in the reign of Edward III., was one of the three principal ports of the island.) Mr. Samuel White has a shipbuilding establishment below the Queen's private landing-place, called FALCON YARD. A floating bridge connects East and West Cowes.

The CHURCH of East Cowes, dedicated to St. James, is a modern building. Her Majesty the Queen, then the Princess Victoria, laid the first stone on the 6th September 1831. It was opened in 1833. In 1868 it was enlarged; and a new chancel was built in 1870. It possesses no very great interest.

The tourist may return to Newport by boat if the tide permits; or keep along the river bank to the Folly Inn, cross to Werror Farm, ascend the slope to Northwood Church, and thence, by way of Parkhurst, to Newport.

NEWPORT to GODSHILL.

The road from Newport to Godshill is one of the most picturesque in this part of the Wight. On emerging from the town—leaving behind us, on our right, the church of ST. JOHN'S—we quickly descend to SHIDE BRIDGE, on the Medina—a spot of some importance in the earlier history of the island—cross the Medina, and traverse the valley that here breaks through the central range of chalk hills. We follow the course of the river with but little variation until Blackwater is reached. Here the valley opens upon a wide expanse of meadows and cornfields, and the undulating downs stretch far away to the east. At the base of Pan Down may be noted the plain brick building of STANDEN HOUSE. To the right extends the well-timbered park of GATCOMBE, situate in a pleasant valley, and watered by the winding river. Observe GATCOMBE HOUSE (Mrs. Estcourt), and the square gray tower of GATCOMBE CHURCH, rising conspicuously above the trees. It is worth making a slight detour to visit the Church, which possesses a charming 15th-century tower; and there are some good Perpendicular windows in the nave, containing some of their original painted glass. The Church was reseated and a new chancel added in 1865 from the designs of Mr. R. J. Cornewall Jones. In the chancel, on the north side, is the old wooden cross-legged effigy of a crusader, of the early part of the 13th century. There is some very good glass in the chancel. In due time we reach PIDFORD HOUSE, about 3 miles from Newport, where a road diverges to Gatcombe, and another road, or lane, a short distance beyond, to Sheat Farm, and thence southward to Chillerton. ROOKLEY and its little schoolhouse is our next point. Here we have a choice of routes. The road to the left skirts the sloping sides of Rookley Down, and passes some sequestered farmsteads on its way to Godshill, affording some fine views of the southern downs, and the distant hill (of ferruginous sand) upon which stands GODSHILL CHURCH. The other road at the *Chequers* Inn divides again,—one branch, by a circuitous route, reaching Godshill; the lane to the right crossing Bleak Down, and proceeding by way of Lashmere Pond and Appleford—an excellent locality for the botanist—to NITON.

Let us suppose that we have arrived at GODSHILL (population 1302. Inn: *The Griffin*). This is one of the prettiest of the island-villages; it is studded with irregular cottages and trim gardens. The CHURCH, dedicated to All Saints, is worth a visit, as well on account of its architectural merits and interesting memorials, as of its admirable and striking position. A fine view is to be obtained from the churchyard. "To the north the gaze embraces the whole of the vale of Newchurch, with the undulating ridge of the chalk downs beyond, ending towards the valley of the Medina in the abrupt slope of St. George's Down. The white cliffs of Culver are just descried over some rising ground to the right; to the left we have the ridge separating the valleys of the Yar and Medina, and the bold line of chalk downs which here take a due southerly direction. To the south the view is more varied. The northern front of the southern chalk range, with its bold projecting spurs and sinuous valleys, lies before us. Appuldurcombe, or Week Down, with its shattered obelisk, bold wall of cliff (the northern face of the firestone stratum, which gives its picturesque character to the Undercliff), and rich hanging woods, rising immediately in front over the scattered houses and leafy knolls of the village; to the west is the huge mass of St. Catherine's, marked by the twin pharoses, and the slender Alexandrian pillar; to the east rises the more picturesque outline of Shanklin Down, with its belt of timber half concealing its cliffs, on the summit of which stands the modern ruin of Cook's Castle."—(*Venables.*)

ALL SAINTS' CHURCH consists of a nave of four bays, with south aisle; chancel and south chapel; north and south transepts; south porch and a western Perpendicular tower, so like to those of Carisbrook and Chale, that it was probably erected by the same architect. On the gable of the south transept stands a singular SANCTE BELL* turret. The porch contains two tablets blazoned with inscriptions —one in Latin, the other a versified translation—in honour of *Richard Gard*, who liberally endowed the village school.

There are many interesting monuments in the interior. The best, perhaps, is the rich altar-tomb, *temp.* Henry VIII., with fretted canopy, of Sir *John Leigh* and his wife *Mary.* The recumbent figures are in alabaster. Notice may be taken of the kneeling figures of Sir *James Worsley* and his wife *Anne;* the memorial to *James Worsley*, captain of the island, d. 1595, and his two sons,—

"Sorte perempti
Prepropera, infesti pulveris igne jacent,"

slain in boyhood by an accidental explosion of gunpowder in the gate-house at Appuldurcombe. In the chancel aisle is a sarcophagus, with busts and figures, erected by Sir *Robert Worsley* for himself and his brother Henry ; and the monument to Sir *Richard Worsley*, the last male of his famous line, erected by the late Earl of Yarborough, who married Sir Richard's niece. There hangs in the church a very fine painting by Rubens of Daniel in the lion's den.†

Godshill was one of the six churches with which William Fitz-Osbert, after the Norman Conquest, endowed the abbey of Lire, in Normandy. Charles I. presented it to Queen's College, Oxford. It was injured by lightning in January 1778.

Dr. Henry Cole, who changed from Protestantism to Roman Catholicism, and back again, according as Mary or Elizabeth sat upon the throne, and who "damn'd himself to everlasting fame" by consenting to preach the sermon when Cranmer was burnt, was born at Godshill.

A day or two here may be agreeably spent in examining this delightful locality. The road to VENTNOR passes SANDFORD (where the *Anthemis Arvensis* occurs), Wroxall,

* This bell was rung, and is rung now in Catholic countries, at the consecration of the Blessed Sacrament in the Mass.

† This picture, formerly in the collection of Sir Richard Worsley at Appuldurcombe, and given to the parish by the late Earl of Yarborough, has recently attracted considerable attention from the fact that a "replica" of it in the Duke of Hamilton's collection was sold at Christy's in July 1882 for 4900 guineas. This picture is considered to be more valuable than that.

and crossing the Downs, suddenly descends to the Undercliff. The walk to WHITWELL and ST. LAWRENCE may also be commended; and an excursion should not fail to be made to Shanklin, by way of Sandford, French Mill, Whitely Bank, and Hungerberry Copse.

NEWPORT TO CALBOURNE, 5½ Miles.

Leaving Newport by the high road for Carisbrook, we pass through that village, leaving Carisbrook Church on the right hand and the castle on the left, and when we get to the top of the village take the right hand road and so gain BOWCOMBE DOWN (Beaucombe, fine valley). In the hollow beneath lies the manor-house of Alvington, and beyond, the dark fir clumps of Parkhurst Forest. At PARK CROSS, 2¼ miles, a road, right, branches off to Thorness, and from thence by Tinker's Lane and Lower Cockleton into West Cowes; another, left, crosses the chalk hills to Bowcombe Farm. Continuing our route we reach (at 4 miles from Newport) the grounds and mansion of SWAINSTON (Sir Barrington Simeon), included in the manor of Swainston, a manor anciently attached by King Egbert (A.D. 826) to the see of Winchester, and retained as the bishop's palace until the twelfth year of the reign of Edward I. The manor was afterwards in the hands of the Montacutes, Earls of Salisbury, the king-making Earl of Warwick, Clarence brother of Edward IV. and his victim, and the Countess of Salisbury, beheaded in her gray hairs by Henry VIII. The countess's grand-daughter received the forfeited estates from the generosity of Queen Mary, and bestowed them and her hand upon Sir Thomas Barrington, from whom they have descended by marriage to their present proprietor. The house, a square stone mansion, about half a century old, contains some Mediæval fragments of the ancient episcopal residence. The demesne is richly wooded. To the north lies WATCHINGWELL, a portion of the old royal chase of Parkhurst Forest. Southward runs a picturesque lane to ROWRIDGE (where, in the neighbouring copses, may be found the beautiful *Calamintha sylvatica*, and on the downs several varieties of orchises), and across the hills to GALLIBURY and ROWBOROUGH, the sites of some ancient Celtic pit-villages.

At a mile and a half from Swainston we gain the interesting village of CALBOURNE (population, 693. Public-house: *The Sun*), partly situated round a pleasant green, adorned by its church and parsonage, and watered by the stream— the CAUL-BOURNE—from which it takes its name. All about this most charming village lie quarries, large and small, of fresh-water limestones, where excellent specimens of the fossils peculiar to these strata may readily be obtained; and the botanist should be on the look out for the *Orchis ustulata*, *Inula Helenium*, *Verbena officinalis*, *Neottia Nidus-avis*, and *Bupleurum rotundifolium*, of which some fine plants are often procurable.

The CHURCH, dedicated to All Saints, is very interesting. It consists of a nave and south aisle, chancel and south aisle, a north transept and a tower at the west end of the aisle, There is a good deal of fair Early English work. The east window of the chancel consists of two lancets with a trefoiled circle above; the east window of the aisle also two lancets with a quatrefoil above. A great part of the tower fell down in 1752, and was then rebuilt as we now see it. In a slab inserted in the pavement of the south aisle is a good brass effigy of an armed knight, *temp.* Edward III., supposed to commemorate one of the Montacutes, Lords of Swainston. A brass plate affixed to the north wall of the chancel is inscribed to the memory of the puritan minister of Calbourne, the "reverend, religious, and learned preacher, Daniel Evance," with an anagram on his name, "I can deal even."

"Who is sufficient for this thinge,
Wisely to harpe on every stringe,
Rightly divide the word of truth
To babes and men, to age and youth.
One of a thousand where he's found,
So learned, pious, and profound—
Earth has but few—there is in Heaven
One who answers, 'I can deal even.'"

A short distance below the church, its grounds skirted

by Lynch Lane (leading to Calbourne Bottom, and across the downs to Brixton), stands WESTOVER PARK, a modern house of no great pretensions, founded by the Holmes family, and now occupied by Lord Heytesbury. The late Lord Heytesbury was governor of the Isle of Wight from 1851 to 1857.

From Calbourne the tourist may prolong his excursion by way of Newbridge (across the Newton river), Stoneover, Wellow, and Thorley, to YARMOUTH, 6 miles; or he may turn aside at Newbridge and proceed through the river-watered meadow to SHALFLEET, 3 miles. Through Lynch Lane and Calbourne Bottom to BRIXTON, $3\frac{1}{2}$ miles, will be found a delightful walk. From Calbourne to Freshwater Gate, 6 miles, is an excursion of great interest and surprising beauty.

NEWPORT TO KINGSTON, *viâ* GATCOMBE.

Six miles of woodland, meadow, and heath; six miles of agreeable, if not particularly striking scenery will be enjoyed by the traveller from Newport to Kingston. As we leave Newport in our rear, the gray walls and conspicuous keep of Carisbrook Castle rise prominently on the hill on our right, and soon we penetrate the orchards of Whitcombe. Just before we enter the park of Gatcombe, we pass, on our left, a lane, leading into the Blackwater road, called SANDY LANE. A romantic road, on the right, leads to the sequestered village of GATCOMBE.

GATCOMBE CHURCH, dedicated to St. Olave, raises its Perpendicular tower above a mass of foliage, and in a dell of tranquil loveliness. A melancholy interest attaches to the stained glass east window of the church. The new chancel, from the designs of R. J. Cornewall Jones, was being built for the then rector, the Rev. J. Branthwaite, Principal of St. Edmund's Hall; and when the walls were just up to the level of the east window, Mr. Branthwaite was accidentally drowned whilst bathing at Morecambe, in Lancashire. The stained glass window was put in as a memorial of him.

GATCOMBE HOUSE is a large stone mansion, built about 1750. "The high knolls of timber that back and flank the building, and a range of coppice that covers the steep precipice of a lofty hill on the south side, sufficiently mark out its beautiful situation."—(*Wyndham.*)

Resuming our ramble, we keep within the shelter of the hollow as far as the old Jacobean manor-house of SHEAT, and then commence the ascent of the ravine which, at CHILLERTON, breaks through the chalk-hills. Turning aside, at length, from the lofty crest of Chillerton Down, the road which we follow strikes into the open fields (lower greensand), passes BILLINGHAM HOUSE, formerly a seat of one of the branches of the Worsley family, and reaches, in a most exposed and bleak situation, the little church of KINGSTON. (Population, 65.) The old church having fallen into utter decay, was rebuilt from the designs of R. J. Cornewall Jones in 1872. The plan of the old church was carefully retained, but a vestry was added. There is some good glass, and a curious old brass of the sixteenth century to Mr. *Richard Mewys*, date 1535.

In the neighbourhood will be found plants characteristic of the lower greensand districts:—Bristle-bent (*Agrostis setacea*), the Knapweed, Ox-eye, *Silene Anglica*, *Filago minima*, and *Tanacetum vulgare*.

NEWPORT TO SHORWELL.

From Newport to Shorwell is 5 miles. The tourist leaves Newport by the High Street and the Carisbrook Road, and passing through the village of CARISBROOK, follows the high-road, having BOWCOMBE DOWN on the right hand.

We pass BOWCOMBE FARM on the left, IDLECOMBE FARM on the right, and after walking just three miles from CARISBROOK CHURCH, reach ROWBOROUGH FARM. Here a little lane turns up from the main-road to the right to an ANCIENT BRITISH SETTLEMENT, well worth examination, lying in the hollow between Gallibury and Rowborough Downs. Another half-mile brings us to the summit of the chalk-range, and we descend into the valley of Shorwell, the road for some distance skirting the grounds of NORTH-COURT (Lady Gordon), a Jacobean mansion, commenced by Sir John Leigh. The terraced gardens are of great beauty, and command some admirable views of the adjacent country, and the waters of the British Channel. In a woody hollow is a mausoleum containing a sarcophagus of white marble in memory of Miss C. Bull, erected by her sister, a former proprietrix. In the grounds rises a crystal spring, which gives name to the neighbouring village.

SHORWELL (population, 622) occupies a position of more than ordinary beauty, with a church of considerable interest. The latter, dedicated to S.S. Peter and Paul, was very fairly restored in the year 1848. It consists of a nave and chancel, north and south aisles—separated from the body of the church by arcades of the fifteenth century—and tower and spire at the west end. A curious fresco, illustrative of the life of St. Christopher, ornaments the wall over the north door. It is in tolerable preservation. The stone pulpit, also of the fifteenth century, with its iron hour-glass frame, *temp.* James I., is interesting. The font is of the same period. In the chancel is a brass of an ecclesiastic of the date of 1518, bearing the following inscription :—

> of yr charite pray for ye sowle of Richard
> Bethell late vicar of ys church of Shorwell
> ye which decessed ye xxiiii day of marche
> in ye yere of our lord m^{t.} d^{c.} xviii on
> whose sowle jhu have mercy :

There are numerous other interesting memorials. Remark especially the singular brass erected by Barnabas Leigh in honour of his two deceased wives,—one died in 1615 and the other in 1619,—with a complimentary allusion to his *third* spouse, then living. One wife is followed by a train of children ; the other stands solitary and childless. Equally worthy of notice is the memorial to Sir *John Leigh*, of

Northcourt, d. 1629, and his great grandchild *Barnabas*, who died seven days after him. The inscription is singular:—

> "Inmate in grave he took his grandchild heire,
> Whose soul did haste to make to him repaire,
> And so to heaven along, as little page,
> With him did poast to wait upon his age."

Attention may also be directed to the memorials to Lady *Elizabeth Leigh*, d. 1619 — "Sixteene a maid, and fiftie yeares a wife;" and *John Leigh*, d. 1688.

The chalice and paten are curious and interesting. The latter was purchased abroad by the late vicar, and is a singular piece of workmanship. Twelve medallions of the Cæsars encircle a representation of Eve's temptation of Adam, which is also surrounded by an emblematic border, allegorising "Musique, Grammatique, Arithmetique, Astronomie, Minerve, and Retorique." The chalice is dated 1569.

From Shorwell the tourist may proceed to BRIXTON, 2 miles, or through Kingston to CHALE, 5 miles, and BLACKGANG CHINE, ½ mile. *Geranium lucidum* and *Campanula Trachelium* occur in the lanes near Shorwell.

NEWPORT, *viâ* YARMOUTH, TO FRESHWATER GATE.

[Shalfleet, 6 m.; Thorley, 4 m.; Yarmouth, 1 m.; Freshwater Village, 2 m.; Freshwater Gate, 1½ m.]

> "Throughout all the isle
> There was no covert, no retired cave
> Unhaunted by the murmurous noise of waves."
>
> KEATS.

The YARMOUTH ROAD diverges from the WEST COWES ROAD near PARKHURST BARRACKS, and traversing the plantations of Parkhurst Forest, passes the ancient farm of VITTLEFIELD, 2½ miles, and at WATCHINGWELL, 3½ miles, passes through a pleasant breadth of green oak-coppices.

For this road we are indebted, it is said, to brave old Sir Robert Holmes—Dryden's Holmes,—

" Holmes, the Achates of the general's fight,
Who first bewitched our eyes with Guinea gold,"—

but its present excellent condition dates from a more recent period. Some agreeable landscapes, enlivened by the many branches of the Newtown river, greet our eyes as we approach SHALFLEET (population, 1050), but, until we arrive at that village, there is really nothing particularly worthy of note. SHALFLEET CHURCH is very interesting. It consists of nave and aisles, chancel, and a vast square western tower. This tower is Norman, the work of the eleventh century, and there is other work of the same date in the church. The north doorway is Norman, and the tympanum is filled up with a curious sculpture of a figure resting his hands on two animals, though some antiquaries will have it that the allegory so rudely carved represents *David contending with the Lion and the Bear*. The remainder of the building is of various dates, but chiefly of the fourteenth century, and its most interesting features are the windows in the south aisle, the chancel-arch, and the arcades which separate the nave from the aisles. There are some rudely sculptured shields, dated 1630, in the south aisle, and a monumental slab on the chancel-floor; the latter, measuring 5 feet 10 inches, is adorned with shield and spear, and evidently dates from the early part of the thirteenth century.

From Shalfleet a very delightful lane leads to NEWTOWN (Inn: *The Newtown Arms*), a scattering of cottages along the shores of a navigable creek. It is worth visiting on account of its peculiar scenery, but retains nothing of its former importance. From the 27th year of Queen Elizabeth until 1832 it was a parliamentary borough, returning two members, and was as "close" a borough as Grampound or Haslemere. John Churchill, afterwards Duke of Marlborough (1678-81), Admiral Sir Thomas Hopson (1705), and George Canning (1793, 1806, 1807), were among its representatives. Certain lanes are still known as Gold Street, Quay Street, and High Street, and are supposed to indicate its former extent.

The first charter of FRANCHEVILLE (as it was originally called) was granted by Aymer, bishop of Winchester in the reign of Henry III.; a market was allowed it by Edward II. It was destroyed by the Danes in 1011, but recovered from the blow. In 1377 it was again devastated, this time by the French, but did *not* recover; though out of the ashes of the unhappy Francheville sprang the borough of Newtown.

The CHURCH, dedicated to the Holy Spirit, is a chapelry to Calbourne. It was erected from the designs of Mr. Livesay, and incorporated a few fragments of an ancient building. In the TOWN HALL, built in 1699, and now used as a schoolhouse, is preserved a silver mace of the time of Edward IV.

Some tolerable fishing may be enjoyed in a branch of the Newtown river, and the botanist will find on its banks several notable aquatic plants. The salterns below the church should be examined. From sea-water, collected in large shallow pans, the salt is procured by a series of evaporating processes.

BRANCH ROUTE—SHALFLEET TO CALBOURNE.

For the sake of the lover of the picturesque we indicate this pleasant ramble. It is equally agreeable whether he adopts the shortest road, and makes his way into Shalfleet by Elm Copse and Stoney Cross, or traverses the meadows by the bank of the Newtown river, turning into the Calbourne road at Newbridge; or, finally, selects a circuitous but more interesting path, and passes WARLANDS— so named from the ancient proprietor, Walleran Trenchard; NINGWOOD, a picturesque old manor-house; and DODPITS, a large quarry abounding in the freshwater limestone fossils.

MAIN ROUTE RESUMED—SHALFLEET TO YARMOUTH.

A mile or so past Shalfleet, and close to the little rural bridge which carries the Yarmouth road across Ningwood Creek, a lane turns aside, on the left, to NINGWOOD FARM. The tourist then turns to the west and passes WELLOW— said to be the site of the "Waltham" referred to in the Saxon Chronicle, anno 1001, as destroyed by the Danes— and following, with tolerable exactness, the course of a branch of the River Yar, arrives, at 10 miles from Newport, at the village of THORLEY, situated in an agricultural district, but scarcely noticeable for other considerations. Its CHURCH is dedicated to St. Swithin.

We pass the church, cross the Thorley rivulet, and quickly reach the shores of the Solent, along which the road now runs, at a slight elevation, commanding some striking views of Lymington river, Hurst Castle, the New Forest, and the general line of the Hampshire coast, and enter the town of Yarmouth.

YARMOUTH (population 779. Inns: *The George, the Bugle*—the former the ancient mansion of Sir Robert Holmes, where he entertained Charles II. in 1671 ; the latter containing an excellent collection of local birds) will be found a convenient *point d'appui* by the tourist who meditates a thorough exploration of the extreme west of the island. It is a decayed town, with an old-world look about it, although it possesses few antiquities. Its position is very attractive : Alum Bay, the Needles, and Freshwater Gate, being within a day's easy ramble ; and to the invalid its clear fresh air must be of unusual benefit. It is more sheltered than Ryde from the keen east winds, and is less exposed than Ventnor to a glaring burning sun.

In the thirteenth century, when it was incorporated by Baldwin de Redvers, Earl of Devon, it was a place of some importance, and much frequented as a port of communication with the mainland. King John visited it in 1206, and again in 1209, on each occasion residing here for a few days. A heavy blow was dealt to the prosperity of the rising town in 1277, when it was burnt to the ground by the French, and a still heavier stroke was its second occupation by the same foe in 1524. A few years later (1539) a round port, or castle, was erected for its protection by Henry VIII. Up to 1832, and from the 27th of Elizabeth, it returned two members to parliament, its representatives being always selected by the Holmes family. The number of electors whose voices were thus expressed in parliament seldom exceeded *nine*.

The trade of the town consists in the importation of cattle, coals, slate, and iron.

The CASTLE commands the entrance to the Yar, and is now nothing but a semicircular battery, armed with four guns. It occupies the site of a church destroyed by the French in the sixteenth century, and some remains of the previous building were incorporated in its erection.

The present CHURCH was erected 1611-1614, by private subscriptions. It consists of a nave, north and south aisles, chancel, and square tower. Some repairs were executed in 1873, and the east window was filled with stained glass in memory of a son of the late rector. In a small projection on the south side of the chancel, stands a remarkably fine statue of white marble (by Rysbrach?), beneath an arched canopy, with solid Ionic columns of porphyry, of Sir *Robert Holmes*, Governor of the Island, 1667-1692, and one of the stoutest seamen of the time. An epitaph in Latin records the principal events of his career; his birth at Mallow, county of Cork; his gallant deeds as a soldier under Prince Rupert and Charles I.; his successes against the Dutch on the coast of Guinea; his capture of the Dutch colony of Nova Belgia, now so famous as New York; his foray in the roads of Vlie, where he burned the villages on the coast, two ships of war, and 140 merchantmen; his attack upon the Dutch Smyrna fleet of merchantmen; and, finally, his long governorship of the island. He was knighted by Charles II. in 1666.

The body of the statue—an exquisite work of art—as well as the sculptor engaged upon it, were captured, it is said, by Holmes on board a French ship. It was intended to be completed with a head of Louis XIV., but Holmes "compelled the sculptor to receive him as a sitter," instead of le Grand Monarque. The rough old seaman conferred many benefits upon Yarmouth ; and the embankment of its marshes was carried out under his direction.

The TOWN HALL, rebuilt in 1764, is a small plain brick building. The NATIONAL SCHOOLS erected in 1855-6, afford accommodation for 220 children.

BRANCH ROUTE FROM YARMOUTH TO FRESHWATER GATE.
(East of the Yar.)

This pleasant ramble will conduct the pedestrian through the little hamlet of THORLEY (see *antè*), and then, in a south-west direction, to WILMINGHAM. Leaving Ham copse on the left hand, at a distance of two miles and a half from Yarmouth, we arrive at the Calbourne road, and turning to the right pass AFTON FARM, and afterwards AFTON HOUSE (B. Cotton, Esq.), a mansion, situated on the hillside which slopes to the Yar. A quarter of a mile more, and we find ourselves in the hamlet of EASTON, from whence a green lane on the right leads to FARRINGFORD, the residence of Alfred Tennyson. Turning to the left, we, however, now pass through the narrow "gate" or opening in the chalk-range, formed by the river Yar, and arrive at FRESHWATER GATE, and the open sea of the English Channel, which here, as Tennyson says,

"Tumbles a breaker on chalk and sand."

A few yards inland, and separated from the sea only by a narrow bank of shingle and pebbles, is the source of the Yar. The river is tidal from Yarmouth to Freshwater Mill, a distance of about two miles.

At Freshwater Gate there are two good hotels : *Lambert's* and the *Albion*. The neighbourhood is famous for its fine chalk cliffs, which near here rise to a height of 490 feet, or as high as Beachy Head, while to the geologist it affords an inexhaustible store of speculation and study.

YARMOUTH TO FRESHWATER GATE. (West of the Yar.)

Instead of adopting the circuitous route through Wilmingham, Thorley, and Afton, which we have just described, we may cross the estuary of the Yar by the bridge, and proceed through the village of Freshwater to Freshwater Gate. On the shore, facing the Lymington river, and commanding fine views of Hurst Castle, the Solent, and the Hampshire coast, is situated NORTON, a collection of cottages and villas. Here are NORTON LODGE (Sir Graham E. W. Hamond-Græme); HILL LODGE; WEST HILL (Major Crozier); AFTON PARK (Benjamin Temple Cotton); FARRINGFORD HOUSE (Alfred Tennyson).

Climbing the hill which overlooks the Yar—at high water the scene is beautiful—we pass through MORE GREEN, and at a distance of two miles from Yarmouth enter

FRESHWATER

(Population 2754. Inn: *The Red Lion*), a very prettily situated village. At its RECTORY was born, July 18, 1635, the ingenious and erudite Dr. *Robert Hooke*, one of the earliest members of the Royal Society, and the great improver of the pendulum. He died at Gresham College, March 3, 1702, and was buried in St. Helen's Church, Bishopsgate Street. Dr. Wood, an accomplished mathematician, was rector of Freshwater; he died in 1839.

The CHURCH is dedicated to All Saints. It consists of a nave and aisles, chancel with side aisles, western tower and a south porch. The nave arcades and the lower part of the tower, which has a singular external arch, are Transition Norman work of the twelfth century. The church was nearly rebuilt in 1876, when a great number of its interesting features disappeared.

The rectory is in the patronage of the Master and Fellows of St. John's College, Cambridge, to whom it was granted by Lord-Keeper Williams in 1623.

In our route to Freshwater Gate we may include FARRINGFORD HOUSE, already referred to as the residence of the author of the *Idylls of the King.* In a lyric addressed to the Rev. F. Maurice he speaks of it pleasantly :—

> " Where, far from noise and smoke of town,
> I watch the twilight falling brown
>   All round a careless-ordered garden,
> Close to the ridge of a noble down."

Mr. Tennyson having been so beset by tourists has built himself a house near Haslemere, and now very rarely resides at Farringford. It may be mentioned that upon the occasion of Her Majesty honouring the Poet-Laureate with a visit at Farringford, the Queen planted a Wellingtonia, as a memorial of her visit. Within a very short time not a vestige of the tree remained—every visitor who got near it carried off a small twig as a relic.

There are many pretty walks in the island which were formerly open to the public, but from which they are now excluded for similar reasons, and because they will not desist from scribbling or cutting their names on trees, gates, fences, and the like.

In the bay, formed by the action of the sea upon the chalk cliffs, rises the ARCHED ROCK, one of two isolated masses of chalk separated from the cliff by natural causes. A similar mass, at no great distance from it, is called the STAG ROCK.

This part of the coast was often sketched by the artist Morland, who made here some of his studies of fishermen, and was accustomed to frequent a small cabaret, " affording every accommodation," says Hassell, " a traveller could wish for "—called THE CABIN (A.D. 1799).

Four-horse coaches run daily during the summer months from Freshwater to Newport and Ventnor.

ALUM BAY, THE NEEDLES, AND CLIFFS' END.

No excursion in the Isle of Wight is probably more popular with tourists than that which we are now about to indicate.

Leaving Freshwater and passing the new FORT, planted on a plateau scooped out of the lofty cliffs, we traverse the ridge of the HIGH DOWNS, rising to the height of 600 feet above the sea, the ridge gradually narrowing as it approaches the Needles Point, where it breaks off abruptly in a bold bluff, overhanging the sea. "The view from hence," says Mr. Thorne, "is glorious, and the balmy breezes come over the wide waters with that delightful freshness which is never felt but in wandering along the lofty hills that rise at once from the ocean. Samphire grows abundantly on these cliffs, and is in common use as a pickle among the poorer classes. The natives are in the practice of gathering the eggs and feathers of the various sea-birds which build in surprising numbers on the ledges and in the crevices of the cliffs. In order to get at these, the men fasten a rope to an iron bar which they have driven firmly into the ground, and then placing themselves on a rude seat formed of two pieces of wood placed across, they lower themselves by means of a second rope, down the face of the cliff."

A LIGHTHOUSE was erected in 1859 on the outermost Needle rock to replace the old one, which was often rendered useless by the thick mists which at certain seasons enveloped it.

THE NEEDLES.

The celebrated Needles are three isolated masses of the extreme west point of the middle range of Downs, which have been produced by the decomposition and wearing away of the rock in the direction of the joints or fissures with which the strata are traversed. The angular or wedge-shaped form of these rocks has resulted from the highly-inclined northward dip of the beds of which they are composed. The appellation *Needles* has been traced by some to the German *nieder fels*, or "nether cliff;" but, more probably, was suggested by the numerous pinnacles starting up from each rugged mass, or by the lofty conical rock, 120 feet high, known as "Lot's Wife," which fell into the sea in 1764, with a crash that was audible at a considerable distance. "There is something imposing," wrote Mr. Rush, the American Ambassador, in 1817, "in entering England by this access." "I afterwards," he continued, "entered at Dover in a packet from Calais—my eye fixed upon the sentinels as they slowly paced the heights. But those cliffs, bold as they are, and immortalised by Shakespere, did not equal the passage through the Needles."

Retracing our steps for a short distance, we may descend the northern slope of the Down by a steep footpath to the WARREN, a broad rugged tract of heath between the Down and HEADON HILL. Behind us may be noted the NEEDLES HOTEL. From the Warren we descend, through a narrow rift or chine, to the shore, after passing the ROYAL HOTEL; then, turning to the left, find ourselves in ALUM BAY. The effect produced by its wonderfully-coloured cliffs contrasting with the glittering masses of the snowy Needles, is very curious and delightful. The strata are vertically arranged, and their tints are so bright and so varied that they have a peculiar appearance :—" Deep purplish-red, dusky blue, bright ochreous-yellow, gray approaching nearly to white, and absolute black, succeed each other, as sharply defined as the stripes in silk; and after rain the sun, which from about noon till his setting, in summer illuminates them more and more, gives a brilliancy to some of these nearly as resplendent as the high lights on real silk."—(*Englefield*.)

Septaria (cement-stones) occur here on the shore, and fossils are also numerous. The *alum* which gives name to the bay is no longer gathered for commercial purposes, but considerable quantities of the white sands found at the foot of Headon Hill are exported for use in glass factories, and the coloured sands, as every visitor to the island knows, are arranged in fantastic forms as pictures or ornaments for sale to curious strangers.

A small spring issuing from the chalk cliff is known as MOTHER LARGE'S WELL; the same old lady's KITCHEN is a cavern at a slight distance farther, which a constant percolation of water renders, we fear, unpleasantly damp.

HEADON HILL, 397 feet (with its new fort), must certainly be ascended by every tourist in search of the picturesque. Colwell and Totlands bays, the valley of the Yar, the wooded lanes and green meadows between Yarmouth and Newtown, Hurst Castle, Lymington, the distant shadows of the New Forest, are included in the magnificent prospect which it overlooks. The geologist will notice here the junction of the chalk with the freshwater deposits and the London clay. The eocene strata, from the uppermost bed in Headon Hill to the chalk, are 1660 feet in thickness.

The relentless speculating builder has recently invaded this hitherto out-of-the-world and picturesque spot, and Totlands Bay is to be transformed into another "rising watering-place." At present it has not got beyond one or two isolated villas, and a couple of shops; but boards with "eligible building lands" are appearing on all hands.

From Headon Hill the tourist may push along the cliff to Colwell Chine. (At Colwell, a few yards inland, is a small Inn, *The Nelson Arms*.) Colwell Bay is bounded, south, by Warden Point, terminating in the dangerous reef known as WARDEN LEDGE. The view from here is very fine. Among the fossils which occur are—the *Cytheria incrassata*, *Neritini concava*, and several kinds of *Cerithia*. Near Bramble Chine are some banks of oysters of considerable extent.

The north extremity of Colwell Bay is called CLIFFS' END, protected by the ALBERT FORT, a battery mounting 40 guns. On the site of CAREY'S SCONCE, a blockhouse erected in the reign of Elizabeth by Sir George Carey, stands VICTORIA FORT, with 50 guns. Between the Sconce and Cliffs' End formerly stood WORSLEY'S TOWER, erected by Richard Worsley, Captain of the Island, about 1544. From hence to Hurst Castle, three quarters of a mile, runs the submarine electric telegraph cable.

The return to Freshwater Gate may be made by way of Norton, More Green, and Freshwater; or from Cliffs' End, through Colwell, Pound Green, Middleton, Farringford, and Easton.

Chillerton

'This way for the Steamers', Cowes

The Parade, Cowes

Newport

St. James Square, Newport

Ryde in the 1920s

A 'magic lantern' projection slide of Osborne House (The Palace of Osborne)

The Sexton, Arreton Church

About the Author, Andrew Gill: I live in Lancashire, England and have collected early photographs and optical antiques for over forty years. I am a professional 'magic lantern' showman presenting lantern shows and giving talks on Victorian optical entertainments for museums, festivals, special interest groups and universities. I am the owner of the Keasbury-Gordon Photograph Archive.

The photograph captions in this album are those printed or hand-written on the original slides or photographs. If you think they are inaccurate or if you have relevant information that I can include in future editions, please contact me.

To purchase prints of selected historical photographs from my archive, visit www.the-keasburygordon-photograph-archive.artistwebsites.com

For a licence to use my historical photographs for commercial purposes, please contact me.

For information about magic lanterns and slides, visit the website of the Magic Lantern Society: www.magiclantern.org.uk

To contact me, email lanternist@ntlworld.com

I have published historical booklets and photo albums on the subjects below. They are available as printed books and ebooks from Amazon. To view all titles, search amazon for 'andrew gill booklets', then click the 'Andrew Gill' link under any title.

Ancient Baalbec   *Ancient Palmyra*   Birkenhead, Port Sunlight and the Wirral   *Birmingham*   Ballyclare May Fair   *Blackpool*   Bournemouth   *Brighton*   Brixham and Dartmouth   *Burnley's Trams*   Cornwall: Morwenstow to Tintagel   *Cumberland*   CWS Crumpsall Biscuit Factory   *Dawlish, Teignmouth and Newton Abbot*   Doncaster   *Eastbourne*   Edinburgh   *Egypt's Ancient Monuments*   Fife   *First World War*   Forth Railway Bridge   *Franco-British 'White City' London Exhibition of 1908*

Glasgow   *Glasgow to Rothesay by Paddle Steamer*   Great Yarmouth
Harrogate and Knaresborough   Hastings   *Hebden Bridge to Halifax*
Holmfirth, Honley and Huddersfield   *Hull*   Isle of Man (5 titles)   *Isle of Skye*   Kentish Coast from Whitstable to Hythe   *Leeds*   Lewes
Lincolnshire   Liverpool   *Llandudno*   London   *Malton, Pickering and Castle Howard*   Manchester   *New South Wales*   New York   *Newcastle upon Tyne*   Norwich   *North Devon*   North Wales: Rhyl to Llandudno
North Wales: Conway to Caernarfon   Nottingham   *Oban to St. Kilda via the Hebrides*   Penzance, Newlyn and the Isles of Scilly   *Plymouth*
Plymouth to Padstow (by railway)   *River Thames from Source to Sea*
River Tyne from Newcastle upon Tyne to Tynemouth   *Rossendale*
Rotherham   *Sarah Jane's Victorian Tour of Scotland*   Scarborough
Sheffield   Somerset   *Southampton, Portsmouth and the Great Liners*
South East Devon   *St. Ives*   Staithes, Runswick and Robin Hood's Bay
Suffolk   Swaledale   *Tasmania*   Torquay   *Totnes and Dartington*
Victorian Childhood   *Victorian Street Life*   Wakefield and Dewsbury
Whitby   York   *Yorkshire Railway Stations*

Printed in Great Britain
by Amazon